GOVERNMENT PROJECTS FOR POVERTY ALLEVIATION

Sulu Province

FROILYN S. JAMAWADI, DPA

GOVERNMENT PROJECTS FOR POVERTY ALLEVIATION

SULU PROVINCE

Copyright @ 2019

By

FROILYN SALLIM JAMAWADI

ISBN 978-621-8307-45-2

Published by

Yawman Book Publishing House

Davao City, Philippines

+639219512458; yawmanwork@gmail.com

TABLE OF CONTENTS

INTRODUCTION

While usually associated with the lack of income, poverty can be defined more generally as a state of want in relation to a social standard. This suggests an absolute notion of poverty that says every person is entitled to a minimum level of well-being, regardless of how affluent others may be. Measuring poverty relative to a poverty threshold or some predetermined consumption standard implies an absolute notion of being poor. The extent of poverty will be higher or lower, depending on how high or low the poverty line is set. Commonly used poverty measures such as the poverty incidence, depth of poverty, and severity are all taken relative to a poverty threshold.

While the Philippines' primary responsibility for reducing poverty rests with the Philippine Government, the international financial community can be a strong ally in alleviating poverty. The scope for improving the effectiveness of development assistance in poverty reduction efforts is enlarged when development institutions consult with their intended beneficiaries and involve the different stakeholders in drawing up the country's assistance strategy. The present poverty assessment, therefore, comes at a very reasonable time. The government is formulating its medium-term development plan with poverty reduction and improved income distribution as the main thrust. A.D.B.'s strategy for poverty reduction in the Philippines must be consistent with the development objectives and priorities of the Philippine Government as spelled out in its medium-term plan.

In 1997, Sulu ranked number one (1) among the ten poorest provinces in the Philippines. In 2000, Sulu ranked number three (3), with Masbate topping the list of the poor provinces in the country. It is noteworthy that in 2003 Sulu registered number thirteen (13), with poverty increasing to 45.1 percent but still one of the 20 poorest provinces in the country. In absolute terms, about 48,195 families in 2003 still live below the poverty line. The income gap of the province of Sulu was placed at 23.0 percent in 2003, lower by 2.3 percent compared to 25.3 percent registered in 2000. The income gap of the province of Sulu was placed at 23.0 percent in 2003, lower by 2.3 percent compared to 25.3 percent registered in 2000. This income gap figure means that on the mean average, the per capita income of low-income families in Sulu is 23.0 percent short of the poverty threshold. The income shortfall of the low-income families was the biggest in Zamboanga del Norte.

Finally, the severity of poverty indicator tries to capture the problem of inequality among the poor. In 2003, poverty was most severe in Zamboanga del Norte province at 16.5 percent. The poverty situation in Sulu, on the other hand, was less severe as it ranked 39th place of the total 85 provinces/cities all over the country with 3.6 percent (Provincial Development and Physical Framework Plan, 2008-2013.)

CHAPTER 1

Underdevelopment among Minorities

Economic underdevelopment and the inadequacy of the education and health services in the south increased Muslim discontent, which inspired the faith of Islam and became a rallying point in the Moro National Liberation Front. It should be noted, however, that on Mindanao and in the Sulu archipelago, the Moros are in the minority, except in the Lake Lanao area (92% of the population) and Tawi-Tawi (94%). During the period of American control, there was large-scale migration from the over-populated plain areas (Visayas, Luzon) to the fertile land of Mindanao, bringing several million Christians into this region. There are now 13 different Muslim tribes in the Philippines the Tausogs and Samals in the Sulu archipelago and Tawi-Tawi, the Magindanaons, Maranaos, Ilanons, and Kalibugan on Mindanao, The Yakans of Basilan, the Higaonons of Cagayan de Oro, the Palawanons and Molbogs of Palawan and the Sangils of the Saranggani Islands.

Poverty lines are applied to income data from the Family Income and Expenditure Survey (FIES). The National Statistics Office (N.S.O.) conducts the FIES every three years. Most poverty analysis begins with the 1985 FIES; subsequent rounds have been in 1988, 1991,1994, 1997, 2000, and 2003. The FEIS is undertaken as a two-stage survey, enumerated in July and January, with reference to the previous six months. Sample sizes have grown with each round, from just under 17,000 households in 1985 to nearly 40,000 in 2000. Headcounts of poverty and subsistence incidence are computed for families and the population. Official documents most commonly report headcounts for families. It is important to be aware of this distinction. The headcounts are lower for families since low-income families tend to be larger. So, for example, the poverty incidence of the population was 34%, while the poverty incidence of families was 28.4% in 2000 [MO3]. 75, the National Statistical Coordination Board (NSCB) releases all official poverty figures. Recognizing that the 3-year gap between FIES rounds was too long to be useful for policymakers concerned with poverty reduction, the N.S.O. launched the Annual Poverty Indicators Survey (APIS) in 1998. The APIS aims to provide access and impact indicators to assess the government's poverty reduction programs. Conducted between the FIES years, the APIS gathers income and expenditure data and information on minimum basic needs classified into survival, security, and empowerment indicators. The questionnaire also elicits some subjective data. The APIS classifies families into two income groupings: the lower 40% of the income distribution (a proxy for those falling below the poverty line) and the upper 60%. to date, three rounds of the APIS have been undertaken:1998,1999 and

2002. The results of the 2004 APIS should be available in 2005 (Poverty in the Philippines: Income, Assets and Access, 1992).

Sulu's economy is still highly reliant on foreign aid. The U.S.A. has not indicated whether it plans to continue pouring substantial development assistance into the region if Misuari is elected over Loong. Still, the U.S.A. Embassy in Manila has insisted that it will respect the result of Sulu's democratic process (Tarrazona, 2001).

With the increasing importance of migration in Asia, governments will need to put in place comprehensive policies designed to maximize migration's contribution to economic growth and poverty reduction. While international migration is often recognized as an important source of foreign exchange, the role of internal migrants is often invisible. Internal migration can serve as one of many livelihood strategies for poor people and a part of the development process. Although both internal and international migrants remit, obtaining an accurate level of remittances is difficult. Available estimates and official data cover only remittances flowing through the formal transfer system and hence underestimate the true level of remittances. They may not also include the amount invested in the countries of origin by businessmen overseas (e.g., the non-resident Indians, the Viet Kieu, and the overseas Chinese).

Nonetheless, available statistics show that amount of remittances virtually doubled from 1988 to 2000 in Asia (figure 1). As most remittances, in cash or in-kind, are sent back to the migrants' family members and relatives, the most obvious impact of remittances is to support the subsistence and income of resident households in the places of origin. Remittances not only increase the individual household income, but a part of them can also be channeled into investments and contribute to the growth of the local economy. The use of remittances for private consumption may even stimulate demand, which may create local markets and jobs for non-migrants.

Although the proportion of total income from remittances may be less in poorer households, the relative impact is like to be greater (Skeldon, 2002.) Among the poor, a large proportion of remittances may be spent on consumption rather than on investment. Remittances also directly increase the household income of those families, in many cases, by over 50 percent of the total household income. Remittances are less volatile than other financial inflows, and their use can have several multiplier effects in the local economy.

Suppose economic development is defined as the realization of higher employment and income levels, high savings and investment, and a steady reduction of poverty. In that case, migrant remittances may be very effective in putting cash directly into the hands of poor people to help them out of poverty. Two mainstream of worker outflow can be identified. The first is permanent migration, in which workers settle abroad for an indefinite time, and the second contract or temporary migration, in which the migrant workers return home upon the termination of their contract; about 7 million Filipinos live and work abroad. Some 3 million out of the 7 million are temporary migrants at land-based contract work. Labor exports are important to the Philippines because of overseas workers' billions of dollars of foreign exchange and the jobs generated by overseas employment.

Moreover, the remittances sent to the country appear greater than flows of development assistance and foreign investment combined. For 15 years (1982-1998), the official remittances sent through the banks amounted to US$ 35 billion. In 2000, the I.M.F. estimated that US$ 6,366 million were remitted to the country. While migrant remittances accounted for only 0.7 percent of the G.N.P. or 16.7 percent of the Philippines' export earnings in 1998 (Tan, 2001). Official statistical data (N.S.O., 2001) showed that 90 percent of remittances were sent overseas.

CHAPTER 2
Poverty among Minorities

Amarta Sen (1995) has suggested viewing poverty in terms of capability deprivation, that is, as "the failure of some basic capabilities to function- a person lacking the opportunity to achieve some minimally acceptable levels of these functionings." (p. 15). This view brings to the fore the concept of human development, which emphasizes that people seek to live reasonably comfortable lives and accomplish more during their lifetime. From this perspective, poverty is the lack of real opportunities "to accomplish more and be more." Islam Rizwanul (2001) pointed out that the diversity of the Asian experience we respect for poverty reduction enables one to draw useful lessons from that experience.

One lesson is the importance of employment and labor market outcomes. As income is an important aspect of poverty, and as productive employment is a key determinant of income, one way of defining pro-poor growth is in terms of the employment outcome of growth. Therefore, decent and productive employment is one of the best routes out of poverty. The record of poverty alleviation in Asia seems better than that of other developing regions (Africa and Latin America). During the 1990s, Asia was the only developing region where poverty (defined as the percentage of people living at less than US$1 per day) registered a substantial decline. Despite this achievement, however, there is very little room for complacency. Asia remains home to over two-thirds of the world's poor. While some countries in East Asia and Southeast Asia have achieved impressive reductions in poverty, the performance of the Southeast Asian countries has been rather modest. Furthermore, the recent economic crisis shows how fragile some of the gains in poverty reduction can be sustained poverty reduction; therefore, it needs to remain a live issue on the Asian development agenda (Islam, Rizwanul 2001). According to CedeŇo (2001), it would take for the average poor to cross the poverty line if no efforts were made to redistribute income and resources. There should be inequitable access to basic services, productive assets, and income-earning opportunities. The need is to find the balance between the delivery of basic services about the need to improve infrastructure facilities so households can directly access basic services and livelihood opportunities. She continues that there are stumbling blocks to the effort of poverty alleviation. The inequitable access to basic services stops the poor from improving their human capital and reduces their chances of exchanging such capital for incomes and other services. Basic forms of human capital are health, a safe dwelling place, clean water and sanitation, proper health care, knowledge, attitudes, values and skills, cultural environment, and social relationships. Some human capital is genetically inherited, but since most human capital that matters are acquired by society, it is a public concern. The inequitable access to productive assets means the inability of the poor to own or control the resources they need to be economically productive.

Based on the data presented in poverty in the Philippines: Income, Assets and Access, 1992, the official poverty measurement in the Philippines is done using two poverty lines: the food threshold and the poverty threshold. The food threshold is a measure of food needs only, and the proportion of people falling below this line is referred to as the substance. People falling below the food threshold are sometimes called the" core poor." The poverty threshold is derived by multiplying the food threshold by a factor representing the average expenditure of the households whose total expenditure is roughly equal to the food threshold. 74 The resulting poverty threshold is known as a lower-bound poverty line. Lower-bound poverty lines are austere, based on the spending patterns of people who must give up necessary food spending patterns of households whose food expenditure is equal to the food threshold.

Banlaoi (1997) explains that when the Philippines acceded to the World Trade Organization (W.T.O.) in 1995, the country demonstrated its determination to face the challenges of globalization. Recognizing that globalization is the buzzword of the 21st century and inevitably affects the growth and governance of many nation-states, the Philippines bravely entered the W.T.O. to prepare itself for global competitiveness and reap the benefits of globalization. Despite its great optimism about joining the W.T.O., the Philippines is still lagging behind its Southeast Asian neighbors in terms of economic performance. Whereas the Philippine economic growth was second only to Japan's in the 1960s, the Philippines is now viewed as one of the sick men of Asia. The Philippines entered the global economic arena with its domestic political economy unprepared. The Philippine state has failed to create the fertile socioeconomic environment that would have prepared the country for global completion.

He further stressed that to bridge the gap between the rich and poor, the Philippine government has formulated a series of medium-term development plans with socioeconomic reform packages. The Philippine government even accepts that successful economic growth and effective governance cannot be achieved without a strategy for socioeconomic reform. However, the Philippine state's weakness is preventing socioeconomic reform programs' implementation. Thus, the implementation of socioeconomic reform programs is a function of institutional reform, as discussed above. The Philippine state is in the predicament of facing globalization while simultaneously undergoing the painful process of nation-building in a highly diverse society. In facing these challenges, the Philippine state is causing pervasive poverty that results in ethnic, socioeconomic, and religious tension. To overcome these challenges, there is a need to strengthen the Philippine state and its institutions of governance through a bureaucratic, electrical, party, and socioeconomic reforms.   In the ESCAP region during the 1990s, poverty appears to have declined in several countries. By the 1990s, many countries' poverty levels had fallen below 40 percent. Although migration is an important phenomenon in Asia, past analyses of poverty have often neglected to account for migration. Migration is related to the lives of the urban and rural poor in many countries in the region. Labor migration and the remittances sent home by migrant workers are now crucial features-if, not determinants- of the rural economy of migration to poverty; current debates pay too little attention to the contribution of migration to poverty reduction. Development and public policies tend to ignore migration or even have the implicit or explicit aim of reducing migration. While innovative programs for migrants have been introduced in many Asian countries, national and subnational development plans currently do not focus on the importance of migration to national development or seek to increase benefits and opportunities for poor migrants (Dang Nguyen Anh, 2003).

CHAPTER 3

Poverty and Migration

Dang Nguyen Anh (2003) confirmed that in an attempt to examine the poverty-migration issues in Asia, this book aims to pave the way for systematic work in this important area and generate some policy recommendations initially. The book examines the extent to which migration and migrants can serve as development resources to assist the poor and reduce poverty. It focuses on voluntary or economic migration, which tends to be most relevant for poor people. This book's fundamental premise is that while population movement is not the only factor related to poverty, migration can significantly contribute to poverty reduction. Four countries, namely Bangladesh, China, the Philippines, and Viet Nam, sharing principal differences and similarities in migration patterns, poverty reduction, political systems, and cultural traditions, are selected for this work. Both internal and international movements are included for analysis. For Bangladesh and the Philippines, the book examines international migration, whereas for China and Viet Nam internal migration is assessed in relation to poverty reduction. They are discussed separately as case studies without attempting to generalize for the region as a whole. Dang Nguyen further stressed that in the traditional viewpoint, migrants are both pushed by a lack of opportunities at home places and pulled by the hope of economic gain. Underlying the movements is a search for a better life. Migration can help achieve this by associating people more closely with available economic opportunities, employment, and services. This thesis is still relevant today. Internal migration to urban centers has been associated with macro-economic growth and represents a significant livelihood strategy for poor people. Rural poor migrating to cities find life there hard, but they can benefit from the movements. Temporary migration is perceived as a way of maximizing the family's income and minimizing its risks (Stark, 1991). An international movement is, on the whole, also contributing to poverty reduction. The monies sent back by migrants contribute more to national and local economies than the trade-in in several countries. About US$ 63 billion go each year to developing economies from migrant remittances. This figure far exceeds all overseas development assistance (ODA).

There is a tight linkage between migration and poverty. Migration can be considered an alternative to escape poverty. It, through remittances, contributes to the poverty reduction, at least at the places of origin. Conversely, poverty creates the premises for the decision to migrate, though it does not necessarily lead to that decision. While migration is both the creator and the product of poverty, poverty may cause immobility as much as mobility (Skeldon, 2002).

Every year about 600,000 Filipinos are deployed overseas. Indeed the services of Filipino workers are the most globalized of the country's economic forces. In the context of economic globalization and rapid advancements in information technology, the high unemployment situation in the country has increased the pressures for labor migration. 6 Coupled with a long history of migration and the migrant networks and culture, overseas migration to work continues to be a viable option and reality for Filipinos (Gonzales, 1998).

Filipino workers were in cash, while the remaining 11 percent were in kind. These remittances were made through banks (67 percent), door-to-door systems (21 percent), and other means (12 percent). Filipino workers in Asia were senders of the highest cash remittance, followed by those working in North and South America, Europe, Africa, and Australia. While the trends of family income and remittances increased over the years, during the 1990s, the remittances were equivalent to twice the amount of the mean family income. This shows the importance of migrant remittances for the people and the contribution that migrants make to foreign exchange and economic development. More systematic analyses should be carried out to highlight the significant roles of migration in employment generation and poverty alleviation in the Philippines. While there is no easy answer to the question og how poverty can be alleviated, various studies now provide a fairly strong indication of the role of overall economic growth in alleviating poverty. In Asia, for example, the countries which achieved notable success in poverty alleviation (viz, the people's Republic of China, Indonesia, the Republic of Korea, Malaysia, and Thailand) are also the ones that attained high rates of G.D.P. growth. It must be noted that a high rate of economic growth is only a necessary condition – not a sufficient criterion in itself – for reducing poverty. The nature and content of output growth are extremely important for achieving this goal (R Islam, 2001). Rizwanul Islam (2001) emphasized in his book that output growth must translate into incomes of the poor for growth to contribute to poverty alleviation. For those employed as wage laborers and salaried workers, the quantity of employment and the rate of remuneration is crucial. For self-employed people, productivity and returns are important, which in turn are influenced by a host of factors, e.g., technology, inputs used, and prices of inputs and outputs. Employment, thus, is the key link between output growth and poverty alleviation. Therefore, monitoring and analyzing the growth-employment-poverty nexus is crucial in the fight against poverty. Employment's role in poverty alleviation is indicated by the contrasting experiences (at least up to 1996) between the more successful countries of East Asia, Southeast Asia, and the less successful ones of South Asia. In the former, high output growth was accompanied by employment growth at a high rate, which in turn led to a tightening labor market and increases in remuneration rates. Countries of South Asia were less successful in achieving such employment-augmenting growth and also less successful in reducing poverty.

CHAPTER 4
Poverty Alleviation

The International Labor Organization (I.L.O.) 's World Employment Report for 1996/97 mentions that between 1986 and 1993, in the countries of East Asia and Southeast Asia, with the sole exception of Indonesia, employment grew at more than 3% per annum, while in countries like India and Pakistan, employment performance was weaker. The contrast in this respect is sharper for employment in manufacturing (Table 1). During 1986-92, in countries like Indonesia, Malaysia, the Philippines, and Thailand, growth in manufacturing employment was much higher than in India and Pakistan. The same is true of 1975-80. During the early 1980s, a recession in Malaysia and the Philippines led to declines in manufacturing employment. Still, these countries were able to reverse that trend with very high growth rates after 1985. Such high rates of growth in manufacturing employment enabled countries like Indonesia, Malaysia, the Philippines, and Thailand to achieve significant structural shifts in employment (in varying degrees), which in turn led to a tightening of the labor market and a rise in real wages-thus aiding the process of poverty reduction.

According to A.D.B.'s next medium-term strategy for the Philippines, 2002-2007, the most recent C.O.S. for the

Philippines was prepared in 1998 before the A.D.B. Poverty Reduction Strategy (hereafter strategy) was adopted in November 1999. Although the existing C.O.S. includes poverty reduction as one of its central themes, it needs to be reviewed to ensure consistency of the remaining programs under the C.O.S. with the strategy.

Based on its appreciation of the emerging socioeconomic scenario in the Philippines, the A.D.B. adopted a new Country Operational Strategy (C.O.S.) in 1998 that emphasized poverty reduction and social development. The strategy would focus on Bank resources to support investment in rural development, provision of basic social services, and management of natural resources and the urban environment. The social development emphasis of the 1998 C.O.S. is a significant departure from the previous A.D.B. strategy (1993) that aimed to accelerate the economy's growth and support an aggressive infrastructure expansion program. During the early 1990s, the country faced severe infrastructure constraints, and the government wanted to overcome this by launching a development strategy anchored on global competitiveness. A.D.B. assistance was therefore instrumental in enlarging the role of the national government in the provision of infrastructure services to the extent that the lending program and the government's fiscal program could sustain.

Poverty reduction was previously adopted as a major thrust of earlier Bank strategies. The 1988 C.O.S. aimed to promote poverty alleviation primarily through employment generation, especially in rural areas, as an integral part of infrastructure programs to promote regional development. the poverty alleviation strategy of the 1998 C.O.S. was a more direct approach that focused on improving families' access to basic social services, obviously responding to the programs and policy advocacy of the government's fiscal program could sustain.

The share of the infrastructure sector, which usually dominated the traditional growth-oriented investment strategy, was expected to go down not only because of the renewed focus on social development but also because of the shift towards greater private sector participation. The Bank's participation was to change from investment support that enlarged the role of the national government to capacity building and policy advice that created the right policy environment for private investment. This strategy for supporting the infrastructure sector indicated that the A.D.B. understood and was committed to the institutional reforms that were being pursued and seemed to be comfortable with the real possibility that lending to the sector could reduce the total level of lending operations to the country.

Aside from the changes in sectoral emphasis, the 1998 C.O.S. also made a strong point about eliminating implementation bottlenecks that seriously delayed donor-funded projects. Most of the factors can be traced to long-standing issues such as delayed project starts, inadequate supervision, and delayed release of counterpart funds. Still, the frequency and magnitude of the disruptions seemed to affect the Philippine portfolio more than it normally did in other developing countries.

The poverty alleviation thrust of the 1998 C.O.S. is mainly reflected in the increased allocation of ODA loans going to the "soft sectors" such as rural development, primary health, and basic education. Given the nature of the problems and constraints that characterize these sectors, solving them requires more than simply infusing additional funds. The C.O.S. correctly recognizes the need to incorporate approaches that would harness a fuller role for local government units and elicit the active participation of beneficiaries in project planning and implementation. The evaluation of programs with closer attention to those that have been undertaken in the past or are still being implemented should lead to a better quality of public expenditures that additional Bank resources can support and that can make a better impact on poverty alleviation (These lessons will be taken up on the preparation of A.D.B.'s next medium-term strategy for the Philippines, 2002-2007).

Angeles (2000) discussed that the centrality of gender, participation, and governance issues in sustainable poverty reduction has long been recognized by international development agencies such as the World Bank and the United Nations Development Programme (UNDP). However, these issues still tend to be treated separately, and it was only in recent years that some attempts have been made, particularly on the part of the Management Development and Governance Division of the UNDP, to connect gender, poverty, and governance issues as its contribution to the Beijing +5 initiatives. As Sally Baden notes, "The current literature on governance tends to conflate goals, and assume positive links between, on the one hand, governance and poverty reduction and, on the other, between poverty reduction and gender disadvantage." (Baden 1999: 27)

CHAPTER 5

Gender and Poverty

Gender and poverty linkages have been re-examined in light of the so-called "feminization of poverty" trend. The "feminization of poverty" could imply any of the following trends. First, a greater number of women are poorer than men. Second, the severity or degree of poverty experienced by women is worse than men. Third, there is an increasing trend of more women falling below the poverty line because of the increased number of female heads of households, etc. The social relations of gender have been pointed out to mediate the differential experience and impacts of poverty on women's and men's lives. Governance and gender linkages have also been articulated mainly, in urban poverty reduction, particularly in the effective delivery of social services and mechanisms of urban administration. Meanwhile, participatory work and development tools identified with Participatory Rural Appraisal (P.R.A.), have been used in poverty assessments to aid poverty reduction efforts. Governance and participation linkages are clearly made in attempts to conceptualize "participatory governance" as "the missing link in poverty reduction" (Schneider 1997), as well as in the use of participatory development tools in organizational capacity-building and improvement of local

24

governance. Gender issues, however, tend to be glossed over in participatory development initiatives when trainers and project planners ignore the social difference and inequalities arising from gender, class, ethnicity, and other factors (Guijt and Kaul 1997, Angeles 2000b).

Moreover, Guilt and Kaul (1997) explain that the relationship between gender planning, good governance, and poverty reduction efforts in Southeast Asian states is explored in this work, using Vietnam and the Philippines as case studies for the period 1986 to 1998. It examines a relatively unexplored question on women and change in comparative Southeast Asian studies: How do state bureaucracies that operate in different political and ideological environments integrate women and gender considerations in their official plans and programs for poverty reduction? In turn, how do women relate to politics when state bureaucracies do (or do not) target them as beneficiaries of poverty reduction policies and programs? This book mainly outlines some of the general issues and comparative insights at the level of national state bureaucracies emerging from a much larger work that explores more systematically the differences and similarities in how state bureaucracies in Vietnam and the Philippines implement poverty reduction programs and plans.

As for the four countries under this work, remittance flows increased sharply during the 1990s. For

2001, these countries (excluding China) received significantly over one billion dollars in international remittances.

The popularity of the Philippines was 78 million in 2001, which increased by about 10 million over six years, placing the county under high emigration pressure. The Philippines is the largest exporter of the workforce in Asia, followed by Bangladesh and Indonesia, and amongst the top labor exporters in the world. The state's intervention in promoting overseas employment accounts for the significance of labor migration from the county. Filipino workers have been deployed to more than 190 countries, Europe, Australia, and North America. The most popular destination region of the overseas Filipino workers is still the Middle East despite its apparent reduced attraction during the 1990s (N.S.O., 2001). In addition, there has been a feminization of the Philippines' overseas labor migration as the number of female workers has continued to outnumber their male counterparts since 1992 (Asis, 2003).

CHAPTER 6
Neoclassical Theory of Development

This book is anchored on the Neoclassical theorist of development. Neoclassical theorists could not, of course, turn a blind eye to the kind of convergence predicted by theory was not occurring, and thus they had to look to some "outside" intervention. Government failures provided an easy out. When neoclassical economists go beyond the fundamentals of resources, technology, and preferences, they focus almost exclusively on government—government impediments to markets prevent the economy from working smoothly. But many versions of such theories are inherently unsatisfactory. In some versions, the government failures are assumed to be exogenous, leaving unexplained why they should be larger in some societies than others. In other versions, political—economy models are used to explain the government failures. In this case, they typically do not explain how or when certainly recommended interventions would overcome the political forces that initially led to the distortions. Surely a pious speech from an outside adviser would seem unlikely to displace fundamental political forces! More broadly, we do well in explaining key aspects of the development process.

Today we recognize that government failures can be critically important. But we also recognize that they need to be, and often can be, explained; with appropriate institutional design, they can even be limited. We recognize, as well, that even without government failures, market failures are pervasive, especially in developing countries. 5 The purpose of this chapter, however, is to go beyond the standard discussion of market failures and development to identify a broad set of basic influences on outcomes. We focus on four: institutions, the distribution of wealth, history, and "ecology"— by which we mean the behaviors of other economic agents with spillover effects. Institutions Neoclassical theory pierced the veil of institutions, seeing through (so it argued) the deeper determinants of economic outcomes- the economic fundamentals. Today we recognize that information and enforcement problems impose limits on economic possibilities that are just as real as the limits of technology. Nonmarket institutions arise in response to those limits and influence outcomes.

But the improvement in those institutions- "good mentions"— may not survive on their own if they require complementary changes in other social institutions. "if the institutional matrix rewards piracy, then piratical organizations will come into existence . . ." (North 1994: 361). There is no teleology— no evolutionary force- ensuring that outcomes will be efficient. If a Nash equilibrium in institutional exist, it may not be efficient. We will provide many illustrations going inside the black boxes of institutions. A major thrust of modern development economics is to shift the boundary between what we block-box (for example, treat as an institutional rigidity).

Early theoretical work that focused on institutional issues and the scope for policy in development attempted to identify specific institutional characteristics of developing countries and incorporated them as exogenous features of models. This was the "structuralist" approach to development; Chenery (1975) is an overview. Later work tried to evaluate policies within the context of articulated economic models that explained the problems the policies were designed to solve. The shift in this boundary has strongly affected our policy views. The chapter provides five examples

Complementarities in industrialization.

Earlier models of the "big push" (Rosentein-Rodan, 1943) simply assumed complementarities in demand so that expectations of low investment could be self-fulfilling.

The implication was that the government should intervene in the industrialization process. Later models developed frameworks in which complementarities were derived as an equilibrium outcome. In some cases, the complementarities were shown not to produce inefficiencies (Murphy, Shleifer, and Vishny 1989: sect. 3) or to vanish once an economy was opened to international trade. But in other cases, complementarities did produce inefficiencies, and there were no easy policy measures to resolve them. For example, there may be no simple way around search costs.

•*Rural credit*

Earlier models simply assumed that rural credit markets did not work well. However, later models derived credit market imperfections from information and enforcement costs. These models implied that standard interventions through credit subside might be ineffective but that institutional interventions could improve credit markets.

•*Labor markets*

Earlier models of urban unemployment treated the urban wage as fixed and therefore argued that it did not reflect the opportunity cost of labor. Later models explained why the urban wage might exceed the rural wage but nonetheless reflect the opportunity costs of expanding urban employment in equilibrium.

•*Saving rates.*

Earlier models assumed that a higher fraction of profits than of wages or rural incomes was saved and that rural incomes should be disproportionately taxed. Later experience demonstrated that rural saving rates could be very high, and theory shed light on institutional influences on saving.

•*Political constraints.*

Political processes are endogenous. Earlier models tended to ignore political processes and assume outside intervention could effectively change policies. We distinguish "deep" interventions, which affect underlying economic and political forces and therefore change policies, from "shallow" ones, which do not and which may make things worse. Modern economic theory and development   A key point is that because wealth distribution affects contracts, incentives, and outcomes in one period, it affects the distribution of wealth in the next. An individual with few assets may be relatively unproductive (that is, relative to his output in entrepreneurial occupations or under high-powered incentive contracts that he could enter if he had more wealth). And if there are many individuals with no or few assets, wage rates will be low. With low wages, individuals with initially low wealth will make low bequests to the next generation.

Thus, an initial highly unequal distribution of wealth may reproduce itself from one period to the next. Banerjee and Newman (1993) show that the effects of an initial highly unequal wealth distribution can last forever and permanently limit growth. Mookherjee and Ray (2000) present an even stronger result, allowing agents to save over their infinite lifetimes to maximize their lifetime utility. Why they ask, do not poor agents save aggressively to increase their productivity in the future? In answer, lenders appropriate the returns to the saving of poor agents entirely, resulting in poverty traps" (Mookherjee and Ray 2000: 1).   History. There are other ways besides the distribution of wealth that history affects economic outcomes. History influence a society's technology, skill base, and institutions. It is not necessarily true that the impact of past events erodes over time. Those events may set the preconditions that drive the economy to a particular steady-state.

If this is the case, development may be easier and harder than previously thought. Under the older theory, "all" one had to do to ensure the development was to transfer enough capital and remove government-imposed distortions. Under the new theories, "all" one has to do is induce a movement out of the old equilibrium, sufficiently far and in the right direction that the economy will be "attracted" to a new, superior equilibrium. Although this may require fewer resources, it may take more skill. Some perturbations could lead the economy to an even worse equilibrium—as, some would argue, may have been the case in certain economies in transition. In this broader perspective, the "deep" fundamentals of neoclassical theory—preferences and technology— are themselves endogenous, affected by the social and economic environment.

CHAPTER 7
Survey

Impact of Government Projects on Minorities
Table 1
Government Projects for Poverty Alleviation

(n=369)

Statements	Frequency	Percentage
1. Agricultural Project	251	68.02
2. Aquamarine Project	124	33.60
3. Water & Irrigation Project	105	28.45
4. Literacy Project	237	64.23
5. Health and Nutrition project	228	61.79

Multiple Responses

Table 1 presents the result of the government projects for poverty alleviation as assessed by the respondents from the various Participating municipalities in the province of Sulu. As reflected in table 4, government projects on agriculture obtained the highest percentage of 68.02. This is a clear manifestation that much of the local government's project was in the agricultural where land cultivation skill training and fertilizers distribution are evident to most of the recipients in the municipalities. However, based on the Barangay Officials' interview, these projects were not sustained due to a lack of funds from the municipal since the allotted budget was used for the other government project. Excerpt from the transcription of the interview:

... In mga nakauna mataud dihil mari pa barangay amun pa-iyanun fertilizer ha manga tau nag-uuma, sah bihaun way na pasal in budget yadtu na nakabutang pa dugaing project sin manga mayor.

The next government project with a high percentage of 64.23 is on Literacy project. This literacy project is quite evident within the municipality's capital town and in the municipality's remote areas. Adult Literacy has been in place for many years as a primordial project in education. The government believes that through literacy, we can make a better place, as quoted during the speech of the governor in the province of Sulu. The next item with a high percentage of 61.79 is the Health and Nutrition project. Many of the respondents have now experienced Health center services through the central government effort of "Sentrong Sigla" project. Even municipalities that provided pumpboat for the health workers to serve on the neighboring island under the municipalities' jurisdiction.

Government projects have the lowest rating percentage of 33.60 and 28.45 for Aquamarine and water and Irrigation projects, respectively. Many of the municipalities don't have potable water and irrigation system. Water scarcity has a problem for many people in the province of Sulu. Many have depended on the rain water for drinking and the farm. In fairness to the government, projects for water development have been initiated; however, due to a lack of water sources, the government diverted the funds into other projects. In addition, people along the coast have constructed a deep well for their consumption; in terms of Aquamarine projects, only a very few municipalities have become the recipients of the Aquamarine projects due to their scope and nature of the place.

The data also imply that the majority of the municipalities in the province of Sulu are not progressively developing due to many factors affecting the implementation of these projects; it is noted during the data gathering that some of the hindrances to the implementation of these projects are attributed to the peace and order situation in the place. Thus it can be inferred that there is a minimal and gradual improvement in the people's socioeconomic status. According to Tarrazona (2001) Sulu's Economy is still highly reliant on foreign aid. The U.S. has not indicated whether it plans to continue pouring substantial development assistance into the region if Misuari is elected over Loong. Still, the U.S. Embassy in Manila has Insisted that it will respect the result of Sulu's democratic process.

The findings are confirmed through the National Statistics Office (N.S.O.) report that in 1997, Sulu ranked number one (1) among the ten poorest provinces in the Philippines. In 2000, Sulu ranked number three (3), with Masbate topping the list of the poor provinces in the country. It is noteworthy that in 2003 Sulu registered number thirteen (13), with poverty increasing to 45.1 percent but still one of the 20 poorest provinces in the country. In absolute terms, about 48,195 families in 2003 still live below the poverty line. The income gap of the province of Sulu was placed at 23.0 percent in 2003, lower by 2.3 percent compared to 25.3 percent registered in 2000. This income gap figure means that, on average, the per capita income of low-income families in Sulu is 23.0 percent short of the poverty threshold. The income shortfall of the low-income families was the biggest in Zamboanga del Norte.

Finally, the severity of poverty indicator tries to capture the problem of inequality among the poor. In 2003, poverty was most severe in Zamboanga del Norte province at 16.5 percent. The poverty situation in Sulu, on the other hand, was less severe as it ranked 39th place of the total 85 provinces/cities all over the country with 3.6 percent (

Provincial Development and Physical Framework Plan, 2008-2013).

Level of awareness of selected ethnic tribe on government projects for poverty alleviation

The level of awareness of selected ethnic tribes on government projects for poverty alleviation in the province of Sulu in terms of (a) localizing sustainable agricultural projects: (b) aquamarine resources projects; (c) water development projects; (d) revitalizing education and development project; and (e) health enhancement and reforms project is presented in tables 5 to 10.

Table 2
Interpretative Values for the Level of Awareness on Government Projects for Poverty Alleviation

Numerical Rating	Verbal Description
4.50-5.00	Very high awareness
3.50-4.49	High awareness
2.50-3.49	Moderate awareness
1.50-2.49	Low awareness
1.00-1.49	Not aware at all

Table 2 presents the interpretative values for the level of awareness on government projects for poverty alleviation to guide the worker in numerical and verbal description in the interpretation of the data using the weighted arithmetic mean.

Table 3

Level of Awareness in Terms of Localizing Sustainable Agricultural Project

Statements	Weighted Mean	Verbal Interpretation
1. Government helps build up an agricultural projects to increase farm production in abaca and copra.	3.17	Moderate Awareness
2. Government desires for every farmer to sustain localized agricultural farms by giving subsidies on coffee and cassava plantation expansion.	2.48	Low Awareness
3. Government extends its assistance through farm-market roads.	2.69	Moderate Awareness
4. Government assists the vegetable production in its locality.	2.63	Moderate Awareness
5. Government subsidizes the planting of fruit-bearing trees.	2.27	Low Awareness
Overall Weighted Mean	**2.65**	**Moderate Awareness**

Table 3 shows the level of awareness of government projects for poverty alleviation as perceived by the respondents in terms of Localizing Sustainable Agricultural projects. For example, items on "Government helps build up the agricultural project to increase farm production in abaca and copra" obtained a weighted mean rating of 2.69, described as moderate awareness. The data imply that the respondents believe that when it comes to government projects on agriculture, much of these are concentrated on abaca and copra farm production since most of the land is cultivated for this purpose. The next item which has the weighted mean rating of 2.69 interpreted as to a moderate awareness is on "Government extends it assistance through farm-market road". Some of the respondents consider the government effort on farm-market road which some of the municipalities in the province of Sulu had constructed road for easy transportation.

Moreover, item on "Government assists for the vegetable production in its locality" manifested a weighted mean rating of 2.63 described as moderate awareness. As disclosed in the finding, the respondents are quite aware of the government project assisting in vegetable production. A low awareness was registered in items #2 and 5: "Government desires for every farmer to sustain localized agricultural farm by giving subsidy on the expansion of coffee and cassava plantation" and

"Government subsidizes the planting of fruit-bearing trees" with a mean rating of 2.48 and 2.27 respectively. It has been obvious that there are very few government projects on subsidizing the expansion of coffee, cassava plantation, and fruit-bearing trees. This further implies that the respondents consider it through peoples' initiative to work on coffee, cassava, and fruit-bearing trees plantation.

The overall weighted mean of 2.65 describes moderate awareness and suggests that the government projects for poverty alleviation in terms of Localizing Sustainable Agricultural project are not evident in most of the localities in the province of Sulu; thus, They have moderate awareness.

Table 4

Level of Awareness in terms of Aquamarine Resources Project

Statement	Weighted Mean	Verbal Interpretation
1. Government expands the construction of fish port and the livelihood opportunities for fishermen	3.54	High Awareness

2. Government acquires Seacraft as means of transportation for Bantay Dagat	3.21	Moderate Awareness
3. Government creates a project for Mangrove Reforestation	3.02	Moderate Awareness
4. Government provides port-harvest facilities (Solar Dyer) for seaweeds farmer.	3.24	Moderate Awareness
5. Government establishes the Aqua-farm development project	2.93	Moderate Awareness
Overall Weighted Mean	**3.19**	**Moderate Awareness**

Table 4 reveals the level of awareness of government projects for poverty alleviation as perceived by the respondents in the Aquamarine Resource Project. Among the constructs under the aquamarine resources project, the item on government expanding the construction of fish port and the livelihood opportunities for fishers obtained the highest weighted mean rating of 3.54 described as high awareness. The data imply that most of the respondents believed that the government had extended its assistance to the anglers, and more projects related to fish ports have been implemented in most municipalities along the seashore. This is evidently supported by the expansion project of the government of the Chinese piers and the main ports of the province of Sulu. The next item that obtained second-highest rating (3.24) is item on "Government provides port-harvest facilities (Solar Dyer) for seaweeds farmer," interpreted as moderate awareness. Based on the findings, it can be inferred that the government has worked on a solar dryer for the seaweeds farmer, which is on its final phase of finalizing the implementation in some municipalities.

The item "Government acquires seacraft as means transportation for Bantay Dagat" established a weighted mean rating of 3.21 described as moderate awareness. This result was an obvious reason that seacrafts known as Bantay Dagat" are visible in the province of Sulu, where the government acquired them through national government assistance and projects. However, the item "Government establishes the Aqua-farm development project" registered a low weighted mean rating of 2.93 described as moderate awareness. However, the respondents are not so aware of whether there are more aqua-farm development projects implemented in the province of Sulu.

The overall weighted mean of 3.19 described as moderate awareness, opines that the government projects for poverty alleviation in terms of the Aquamarine Resources Project are not properly oriented in most of the municipalities in the province of Sulu.

Table 5

Level of Awareness in terms of Water Development Project

Statement	Weighted Mean	Verbal Interpretation
1. Government repairs and improves the ten Units Deep Well.	2.95	Moderate Awareness
2. Government constructs and develops water supply system.	3.05	Moderate Awareness
3. Government constructs potable water system	2.77	Moderate Awareness
4. Government provides floating water tank system	2.37	Low Awareness
5. Government provides drilling equipment for level III water supply project	2.11	Low Awareness
Overall Weighted Mean	**2.64**	**Moderate Awareness**

Table 5 reveals the level of awareness of government projects for poverty alleviation as prescribed by the respondents regarding a water development project. Most of the items on water development projects obtained low weighted mean ratings, such as "Government repairs and improves the Ten Units Deep Well" (2.95), "
"Government constructs potable water system" (2.77) "Government provides floating water tank system" (2.37), and "Government provides drilling equipment for level III water supply project" (2.11). The data divulges that the water development projects in most of the municipalities are considered a pressing problem where most of the people in the province of Sulu are looking forward to having in their municipalities. Furthermore, some people depend so much on rain water for drinking and to water their farm plantations.

The Overall weighted mean rating of 3.19 interpreted as moderate awareness, evokes that the government projects for poverty alleviation in terms of the water development project are insufficient in most of the municipalities in the province of Sulu.

Table 6

Level of Awareness in terms of Revitalizing Education and Development Project

Statements	Weighted Mean	Verbal Interpretation
1. Government renovates some classrooms of elementary school buildings.	3.56	High Awareness
2. Government establishes a preschool center and daycare center	3.56	High Awareness
3. Government develops computer literacy and accessibility to information	2.20	Low Awareness
4. Government constructs the provincial library	2.01	Low Awareness
5. Government helps on teacher's enhancement training program	2.16	Low Awareness
Overall Weighted Mean	**2.66**	**Moderate Awareness**

Table 6 reveals the level of awareness on government projects for poverty alleviation as perceived by the respondents in terms of revitalizing education and development projects. Items # 1 and 2 on "Government renovates some classrooms of elementary school buildings" and "Government establishes a preschool center and day care center" manifested the same weighted mean rating of 3.56 interpreted as high awareness. Most of the government priority projects are geared toward renovating classrooms and establishing a preschool and daycare center in most of the localities in the province of Sulu. Department of Education supports this through the government-initiated project on school building improvements implemented in almost all municipalities.

However, items on "Government develops computer literacy and accessibility to information", "Government helps on teacher's enhancement training program, "and "Government constructs the provincial library" with weighted mean ratings of 2.20, 2.16, and 2.01, respectively. As disclosed in the findings, projects such as computer literacy, library construction, and even teacher's training program have not yet been given priority by the government since there are still more urgent problems than the projects mentioned above.

The overall weighted mean rating of 2.66 interpreted as moderate awareness, imply that the government projects for poverty alleviation in terms of revitalizing education and development project is not well implemented in some of the municipalities in the province of Sulu.

Table 7

Level of Awareness in terms of Health Services Enhancement and Reform Project

Statements	Weighted Mean	Verbal Interpretation
1. Government provides the health enhancement and reforms for the people	3.29	Moderate awareness
2. Government expands and improves the municipal hospital and its health-related services.	2.19	Low awareness
3. Government constructs the health centers and nutrition posts.	3.34	Moderate Awareness
4. Government acquires the sea transport (pump boat) for the health personnel working in remote island.	2.48	Low Awareness
5. Government constructs the communicable ward and provides medical facilities and equipments.	2.48	Low Awareness
Overall weighted mean	**2.90**	**Moderate Awareness**

Table 7 discloses the result of the level of awareness of government projects for poverty alleviation as perceived by the respondents in terms of health service enhancement and reform projects. Among the items under the health service enhancement and reform project, item "Government constructs the health centers and Nutrition post" obtained a highest weighted mean rating of 3.34, described as moderate awareness. As part of the department of health government projects, health centers called Sentrong Sigla "have been implemented in almost all municipalities in the province of Sulu. The next item is "Government provides the health enhancement and reforms for the people" with a weighted mean rating of 3.29, described as moderate awareness. The data imply that the health enhancement and reforms for the people are not well distributed throughout most of the municipalities. While items #4 and 5 on "Government acquires the Sea transport (pump boat) for the health personnel working in remote island" and government constructs the communicable ward and provides medical facilities and equipment: obtained the same weighted mean ratings of 2.48 described as low awareness. As revealed in the finding, this implies that projects like acquiring a pump boat for the health workers rendering service in most remote islands and constructing communicable wards, medical facilities, and equipment are not implemented in almost all municipalities. In fact, in the province of Sulu, this is one of the huge problems that the people have been facing for quite some time; thus, many people don't receive any medical services in their municipalities.

The overall weighted mean rating 2.90 interpreted as moderate awareness, imply that the government projects for poverty alleviation in terms of health service enhancement and reform project is not enough for the entire people of Sulu province.

Table 8

Summary Table in the Level of Awareness of the Government Projects for Poverty Alleviation

Statement	Weighted Mean	Verbal Interpretation
Sustainable Agricultural Project	2.65	Moderate Awareness
Aquamarine Resources Project	3.19	Moderate Awareness
Water Development Project	2.65	Moderate Awareness
Revitalizing Education and Development Project	2.66	Moderate Awareness
Health Services Enhancement and Reforms Project	2.90	Moderate Awareness
Overall Weighted Mean	**2.81**	**Moderate Awareness**

The summary table 11 shows the overall awareness of government projects for poverty alleviation as perceived by the respondents based on the identified indicators. All of these indicators registered an overall weighted mean rating of 2.81, considered moderate awareness. However, as shown in Table 11, most government projects are unaware to the people in the province of Sulu. This further implies that the people have not received any government projects for poverty alleviation; thus, most people live within the poverty line.

The data from N.S.O. confirm that in 1997, Sulu ranked number one (1) among the ten poorest provinces in the Philippines. In 2000, Sulu ranked number three (3), with Masbate topping the list of poor provinces in the country. It is noteworthy that in 2003 Sulu registered number thirteen (13), with poverty incidence going down at 45.1 percent, but it is still one of the 20 poorest provinces in the country. In absolute terms, about 48,195 families in 2003 still lived below the poverty line. The income gap of the province of Sulu was placed at 23.0 percent in 2003, lower by 2.3 percent compared to 25.3 percent registered in 2000. This income gap figure means that, on average, the per capita income of low-income families in Sulu is 23.0 percent short of the poverty threshold.

This is corroborated by the book by Islam, Rizwanul (2001) that the record of poverty alleviation in Asia seems better than that of other developing regions (Africa and Latin America). During the 1990s, Asia was the only developing region where the incidence of poverty (defined as the percentage of people living at less than U.S. $ 1 per day) registered a substantial decline. Despite this achievement, however, there is very little room for complacency. Asia remains home to over two-thirds of the world's poor. And within Asia, there is a wide variation in the progress of reducing poverty. While some countries in East Asia and Southeast Asia have achieved impressive reductions in poverty, the performance of the South Asian countries has been rather modest. Furthermore, the recent economic crisis shows how fragile some of the gains in poverty reduction can be sustained poverty reduction therefore, it needs to remain a live issue on the Asian development agenda (Islam, Rizwanul 2001).

Table 9

Differences in the level of awareness in terms of Gender

Variable	Over all Weighed Mean		t-value	P<.05	Decision on Ho
	Male	Female			
Sustainable Agricultural Project	2.54	2.76	-2.097	.037 S	Reject
Aquamarine Resources Project	3.11	3.27	-1.789	.074 NS	Accept
Water Development Project	2.57	2.72	-1.345	.179 NS	Accept
Revitalizing Education and Development Project	2.58	2.74	-1.835	.067 NS	Accept
Health Services Enhancement and Reform Project	2.84	2.97	-1.44	.150 NS	Accept
Total	**2.73**	**2.89**	**-1.701**	**.101 NS**	**Accept**

Table 9 presents the result of the t-test independent sample in the level of awareness of the government project for poverty alleviation when the respondents are categorized according to their gender. A significant difference exists in the respondents' perception regarding sustainable agricultural projects between males and females with the t=-2.097 at α=0.05 probability level with *P* value of .037, which is less than the designated α of 0.05. Therefore, the posited hypothesis is rejected that there is a significant difference among the variables tested in the work. This implies that the respondents differ in their awareness of the government project for poverty alleviation when categorized according to their gender. This further implies that the female respondents have a higher awareness of government projects on sustainable agricultural projects since most of these projects are an incline to horticulture, where women's involvement is quite evident.

However, as revealed in table 9, a significant difference does not exist among the variables in the government projects such as the Aquamarine resources Project with t=-1.789, Water Development Project with t=-1.345, Revitalizing Education and Development Project with t= -1.835, and Health Services Enhancement and reform Project with t=-1.444 and all the *P* values are more than the α of 0.05. Therefore, the posited hypothesis is accepted that no significant difference exists among the variables tested in the work. This implies that the respondents do not differ in their awareness of the government project for poverty alleviation when they are categorized according to gender. This can be inferred that both males and females have almost the same level of awareness of the abovementioned government projects.

In summary, the respondents have not experienced many of the government projects for poverty alleviation as implemented in various municipalities of the province of Sulu; thus, they have a moderate level of awareness since most of the government projects are not yet implemented.

Table 10

Difference in the Level of Awareness in terms of ethnic tribe

Variable	Overall weighted mean			F-Value	P<.05	Decision on Ho
	Tauso g	Sama	Badj ao			
Sustainable Agricultural Project	2.84	2.66	1.87	28.773	.000 S	Reject
Aquamarine Resources project	3.42	2.49	2.65	45.254	.000 S	Reject
Water Development Project	2.91	2.29	1.83	33.680	.000 S	Reject
Revitalizing Education and Development Project	2.87	2.59	1.89	41.246	.000 S	Reject
Health Services Enhancement and reform Project	2.99	2.74	2.66	4.496	.012 S	Reject
Total	**3.01**	**2.55**	**2.18**	**30.69**	**.0002 S**	**Reject**

*Significant at 0.05 level of significance

As observed in table 10, the result of the One-Way Analysis of Variance in the level; of awareness of the government project for poverty alleviation when the respondents are categorized according to their ethnic tribe. As disclosed in the findings, a significant difference does exist among the perception of the respondents in the level of awareness of the government projects for poverty alleviation as they are grouped according to their ethnic tribe in terms of sustainable agriculture with the F=28.773, Aquamarine Resources Project with F=45.254, Water development Project with F= 33.680, Revitalizing Education and Development Project with F=41.246, and Health Services Enhancement and Reform Project with F=4.496 and all the P values are less than the α of 0.05. Therefore, the posited hypothesis is rejected that there is a significant difference among the variables tested in the work. This is evidently supported by the mean ratings of 3.01 for the Tausog and followed by Sama and Badjao with mean ratings of 2.55 and 2.18 respectively in terms of the government projects for poverty alleviation. This implies when the respondents are grouped according to their ethnic tribe, their level of awareness of the government project for poverty alleviation varies from each other. Furthermore, among the selected ethnic tribe, the tausog have a high level of awareness as compared to Sama and

Badjao. This can be inferred that the tausog have felt much of the government projects for poverty alleviation.

Table 11

Difference in the Level of awareness in terms of Educational Attainment

Variable	Overall weighed Mean							F-Value	P< .05	Decision on Ho
	NFS	EL	EG	HSL	HSG	CL	CG			
Sustainable Agricultural Project	1.81	2.31	2.53	2.80	3.12	2.95	2.72	7.858	.000 S	Reject
Aquamarine Resources Project	2.21	3.12	3.38	2.98	3.42	3.09	3.45	7.927	.000 S	Reject
Water Development Project	2.13	2.18	2.39	2.62	2.74	2.92	3.29	10.14	.000 S	Reject
Revitalizing Education and Development project	1.93	3.33	2.41	2.48	2.79	2.89	3.24	14.12	.000 S	Reject
Health Services Enhancement and Reform Project	2.22	2.84	3.03	2.66	2.89	2.86	3.30	5.838	.000 S	Reject
Total	2.06	2.76	2.75	2.71	2.99	2.94	3.20	9.177	.000 S	Reject

*Significant at 0.05 level of significance

Legend:

NFS- No formal Schooling

HSL- High School Level

EL- Elementary Level

HSG- High School Graduate

EG- Elementary Graduate

CL- College Level-

CG- College Graduate

Table 11 presents the result of the One-Way Analysis of Variance in the level of awareness of the government project for poverty alleviation when the data are analyzed according to the respondents' educational attainment. As divulged in the findings, a significant difference does exist among the perception of the respondents in the level of awareness of the government projects for poverty alleviation as they grouped according to their educational attainment in terms of sustainable agricultural with the F= 7.858, Aquamarine Resources Project with F= 7.927, Water Development project with F= 10.142, Revitalizing Education and Development Project with F= 14.128, and Health Services Enhancement and Reform Project with F= 5.838 and all the *P* Values are less than the α of 0.05. Therefore, the posited hypothesis is rejected that there is a significant difference among the variables tested in the work. This is supported by the mean ratings of 3.20 for the respondents who obtained college degrees. This is followed by high school graduates with a mean rating of 2.99, the college level respondents with a mean rating of 2.94, elementary level with a mean rating of 2.76, elementary graduates with a mean rating of 2.75, high school level with a mean rating of 2.71, and respondents with no formal schooling with a mean rating of 2.06. This implies when the respondents are grouped according to their educational attainment, their level of awareness of the government project for poverty alleviation varies from each other. Furthermore, respondents with high educational attainment are more aware of the government projects for poverty alleviation than those with low educational attainment.

Table 12

Difference in the level of awareness in terms of Socio-Economic Status

Variable	Over all Weighed Mean				F-value	P<.05	Decision on Ho
	Below 5,000	5,000-15,000	16,000-25,000	25,000 & above			
Sustainable Agricultural Project	2.58	2.82	2.81	2.15	1.757	.155 NS	Accept
Aquamarine Resources Project	3.12	3.36	3.07	3.45	2.259	.081 NS	Accept
Water Development Project	2.45	3.08	2.85	3.30	9.586	.000 S	Reject
Revitalizing Education and Development Project	2.54	2.89	3.01	2.95	4.860	.003 S	Reject
Health Services Enhancement and Reform Project	2.86	3.01	2.68	3.10	1.170	.321 NS	Accept
Total	2.71	3.03	2.88	2.99	3.93	.112	Accept

*Significant at 0.05 level of significance

*Significant at 0.05 level of significance

Table 12 presents the one-way analysis of variance in the level of awareness of the government project for poverty alleviation when data are analyzed according to the respondents' socioeconomic status. A significant difference exists among the respondents' perceptions regarding the water development project with the F=9.586 and the Revitalizing Education and Development Project with F=4.860, with P value of .000 and .003, respectively, respectively which are less than the designated α of 0.05. Therefore, the posited hypothesis is rejected that there is a significant difference among the variables tested in this work. This implies that the respondents differ in their level of awareness of the government project for poverty alleviation when they are categorized according to their socioeconomic status. This Further implies that the respondents who earned Php 25,000 and above registered a high level of awareness in terms of two government projects, the water development project and revitalizing education and development project. These two projects are more likely implemented in some of the areas of the various municipalities in the province of Sulu, where the respondents have high incomes.

However, as revealed in table 15, a significant difference does not exist among the variables in the government projects such as sustainable agricultural project with F=1.757, Aquamarine Resources Project with F=1.170, and *P* values are more than the α of

0.05. Therefore, the posited hypothesis is accepted that no significant difference exists among the variables tested in the work. This implies that the respondents do not differ in their awareness of the government project for poverty alleviation when they are categorized according to their socioeconomic status based on the abovementioned projects.

In general, the respondents have not experience much of the government projects for poverty alleviation as implemented in various municipalities of the province of Sulu.

Table 13

Difference in the level of Awareness in Terms of Age

Variable	Over all Weighed Mean				F-value	P<.05	Decision on Ho
	20-25 years old	26-30 years old	31-40 years old	41 years old & above			
Sustainable Agricultural Project	2.59	2.73	2.58	2.74	.672	.569 NS	Accept
Aquamarine Resources Project	3.17	3.25	3.25	3.09	.620	.603 NS	Accept
Water Development Project	2.73	2.79	2.46	2.59	1.662	.175 NS	Accept
Revitalizing Education and	2.59	2.82	2.57	2.74	1.788	.149 NS	Accept

Development Project							
Health Services Enhancement and Reform Project	2.86	3.04	2.82	2.91	1.090	.353 NS	Accept
Total	**2.78**	**2.93**	**2.74**	**2.81**	**1.1664**	**.369 NS**	**Accept**

*Significant at 0.05 level of significance

As observed in Table 16, the one-way analysis of variance results in the awareness of the government project for poverty alleviation when the respondents are categorized according to their ethnic tribe. As disclosed in the findings, a significant difference does not exist among the perception of the respondents in the awareness of the government projects for poverty alleviation as they are grouped according to their age in terms of sustainable agriculture with the F=.672, Aquamarine Resources Project with F=.620, Water Development Project with F=1.662, Revitalizing Education and Development project with F=1.788, and Health Services Enhancement and Reform project with F= 1.788, and Health Services Enhancement and Reform Project with F= 1.090 and all the P values are more than the α of 0.05. Therefore, the posited hypothesis is accepted that no significant difference exists among the variables tested in this work. This implies that when the respondents are grouped according to their age, their awareness of government projects for poverty alleviation does not vary. Furthermore, almost all respondents, regardless of their age bracket, have moderate awareness of all the government projects for poverty alleviation.

Bibliography

Cedneño, L., (2001). Quest for peace, Busybook Distributors, 2219 C.M Recto Ave., Sampaloc Manila

Alam, Mustafa (1989), "Special Employment Program in Bangladesh- An Evaluation of Major Schemes."

Betcherman, Gordon and Rizwanul Islam (eds.) (2000), *East Asian Labor Markets and the Economic Crisis: Impacts, Responses, and Lessons*. World Bank and International Labor Organization.

Edita Tan, "Measuring Poverty in Education." Growth, Poverty, and Income Inequality in the Philippines, A. Balisacan and S. Fujisaki (eds.), Institute of Developing Economies, Tokyo 1998.

Gaiha, Raghav (1996), "How Dependent are the Rural Poor on the Employment Guarantee Scheme in India?" *The Journal of Development Studies*, Vol. 32, No. 5, June 1996.

Hossain, M. (1984), "Credit for Alleviation of Rural Poverty: An Assessment of Initial Experiences of the Grameen Bank in Bangladesh," BIDS, Dhaka.

International Labor office (1999), *Indonesia Strategies for Employment- Led Recovery and*

Reconstruction, Report of an I.L.O. mission, Geneva and Jakarta. (1996), World Employment Report 1996/97, Geneva.

Leonora C. Angeles. WOMEN, BUREAUCRACY AND THE GOVERNANCE OF POVERTY IN SOUTHEAST ASIA: INTEGRATING GENDER AND PARTICIPATORY GOVERNANCE IN POVERTY REDUCTION PROGRAMS IN THE PHILIPPINES AND VIETNAM, Center for Human Settlements university of British Columbia, Book presented at the DEVNET international conference on "Poverty, Prosperity, Progress", university of Victoria, Wellington, New Zealand, 17-19 November 2000.

-SAAT (1996), "Nepal: Programs and Strategies for Employment Promotion,"
ILO-SAAT, New Delhi.

Transport Infrastructure and Capacity Development Project (TA No. 2968), prepared by Halcrow Fox for The Government of the Philippines with support from the Asian Development Bank, December 1999, Volume 2: Main Text.6

William F. Fox, Strategic Options for Urban Infrastructure Management, Published for the

Urban Management Program, Washington, D.C., 1994, p.19.

Khan, A.R (1997), "Macroeconomic Policies and Poverty: An Analysis of the Experience of ten Asian Countries," ILO-SAAT, *Alleviating Poverty in Asia*, I.L.O., New Delhi.

Islam, Rizwanul (1990), "Rural poverty, growth and macroeconomic Policies: The Asian Experience," International Labor Review, Vol.129, No.6.

-(1984), "Non-farm Employment in Rural Asia: Dynamic Growth or Proletarianization? "Journal of Contemporary Asia, Vol. 14, No.3, 1984.

- (ed.) (1987), Rural Industrialization and Employment in Asia, ILO-ARTEP, New Delhi, 1987.

Lee, Eddy (1998), The Asian Financial Crisis: The Challenge for Social Policy, I.L.O., Geneva. Lipton, Michael (1998), Successes in Anti-Poverty, I.L.O. Geneva.

Masum, M (1996), "Micro Interventions for alleviation of Poverty in Bangladesh," Unpublished Book, ILO-SAAT, New Delhi.

Muqtada, M. (1989), "The Elusive Target," ILO-ARTEP, New Delhi. Rath, N. (1985), " Garibi Hatao: Can IRDP Do it? *Economic and Political Weekly*, 9 February 1985.

Rodgers, Gerry (1995), *New Approaches to Poverty Analysis and Policy*, Vol.I. I.L.O., Geneva

Senanayake, S.M.P., et al., (1989), "Self-Employement Promotion in Sri Lanka- A Primary Level Investigation of Selected Programs," Muqtada (1989).

Shand, Richard (ed.) (1986), *Off-Farm Employment in the Development of Rural Asia,* Australian National University, Canberra.

Thamarajakshi, R. (1996), "Micro Interventions for Poverty Alleviation Country Work: India, "Unpublished Book, ILO-SAAT, New Delhi.

R. ISLAM... Poverty Alleviation, Employment and Labor Market:

Lessons from the Asian Experience and Policies 22- (1997), "Micro Interventions for Poverty Alleviation in South Asia and East Asia," Book presented at an I.L.O. Workshop on Poverty Alleviation in Bangkok, 5-7 February 1997.

World Bank: World Development Report, Various years.

- (1994), *World Development Report on Infrastructure Development*, Washington, D.C.

- (1996), *Global Economic Prospects and the Developing Countries* 1996, Washington, D.C.

Presidential Commission to Fight Poverty, A National Strategy to Fight poverty, prepared for PCFP by the Philippine Institute for Development Studies with support from the U.N. joint Consultative Group on Policy, 1995, p.46.

Tarrazona, Noel, (2007) Poverty Stricken Community, Asia Times Online Ltd., Zamboanga City

Provincial Development and Physical Framework Plan of Sulu Province, 2008-2013

World Bank, Philippines Social Expenditure management Priorities, Report No. 18562-PH, November 13, 1998.